CARL
EDWARDS

by Connie Colwell Miller

NASCAR
HEROES

Published by ABDO Publishing Company, PO Box 398166, Minneapolis, MN 55439. Copyright © 2013 by Abdo Consulting Group, Inc. International copyrights reserved in all countries. No part of this book may be reproduced in any form without written permission from the publisher. SportsZone™ is a trademark and logo of ABDO Publishing Company.

Printed in the United States of America,
North Mankato, Minnesota
102012
012013

Editor: Chrös McDougall
Series Designer: Becky Daum

Photo Credits: Mike McCarn/AP Images, cover, 26-27; Russell LaBounty/ Autostock/AP Images, cover; Glenn Smith/AP Images, 4-5, 20-21, 30 (middle); Phil Cavali/AP Images, 6-7; Greg Suvino/AP Images, 7; Andre Jenny/Alamy, 8-9; J. Pat Carter/AP Images, 10-11, 22-23, 31; Ed Zurga/AP Images, 12-13; Harold Hinson/Sporting News/Getty Images, 14; Brad Wilder/WireImage/ Getty Images, 15; Tim Sharp/AP Images, 16-17; Ric Field/AP Images, 18-19; Cal Sports Media/AP Images, 24-25, 28-29, 30 (top and bottom)

Cataloging-in-Publication Data
Colwell Miller, Connie.
 Carl Edwards / Connie Colwell Miller.
   p. cm. -- (NASCAR heroes)
Includes bibliographical references and index.
ISBN 978-1-61783-662-6
1. Edwards, Carl, 1979- --Juvenile literature. 2. Stock car drivers--United States--Biography--Juvenile literature. I. Title.
796.72092--dc21

[B]

2012946245

CONTENTS

Carl Edwards Flips Out 4

Born to Race 8

Discovered! 12

A Big First Year 17

The Race Goes On 19

A True Superstar 24

More to Come 27

Timeline 30
Glossary 31
Index 32

CARL EDWARDS FLIPS OUT

Carl Edwards zoomed around the Atlanta Motor Speedway on March 20, 2005. The tires on his No. 99 Ford Taurus were nearly bald. Still, he fought for the lead. With less than one lap left, Edwards edged out the leading car. He tore across the finish line for the win.

FAST FACT
Fans of Carl Edwards call themselves "Edheads."

Carl Edwards (99) edges Jimmie Johnson (48) in 2005 to win his first Cup Series race.

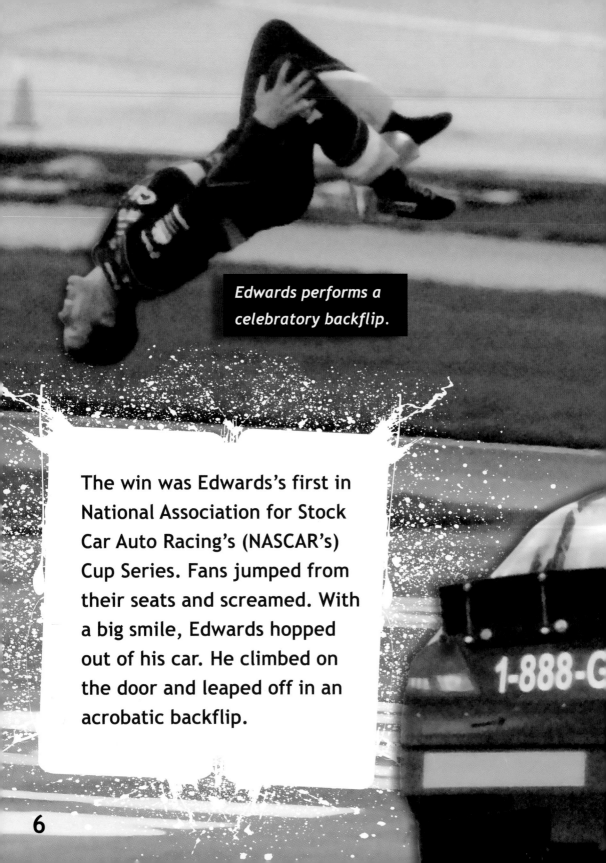

Edwards performs a celebratory backflip.

The win was Edwards's first in National Association for Stock Car Auto Racing's (NASCAR's) Cup Series. Fans jumped from their seats and screamed. With a big smile, Edwards hopped out of his car. He climbed on the door and leaped off in an acrobatic backflip.

Edwards celebrates his first win in NASCAR's Cup Series.

ET-CHARTER 60

Ford

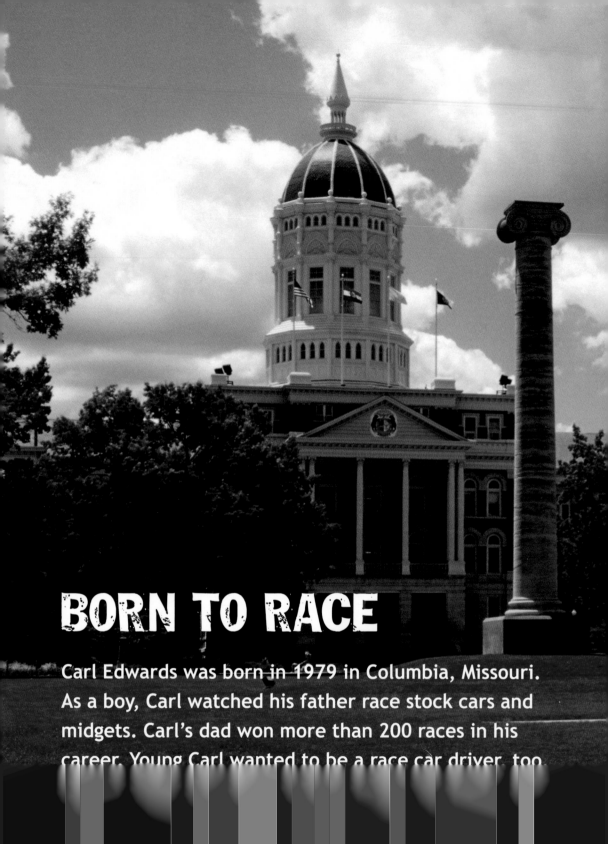

BORN TO RACE

Carl Edwards was born in 1979 in Columbia, Missouri. As a boy, Carl watched his father race stock cars and midgets. Carl's dad won more than 200 races in his career. Young Carl wanted to be a race car driver, too.

Carl attended the University of Missouri in his hometown.

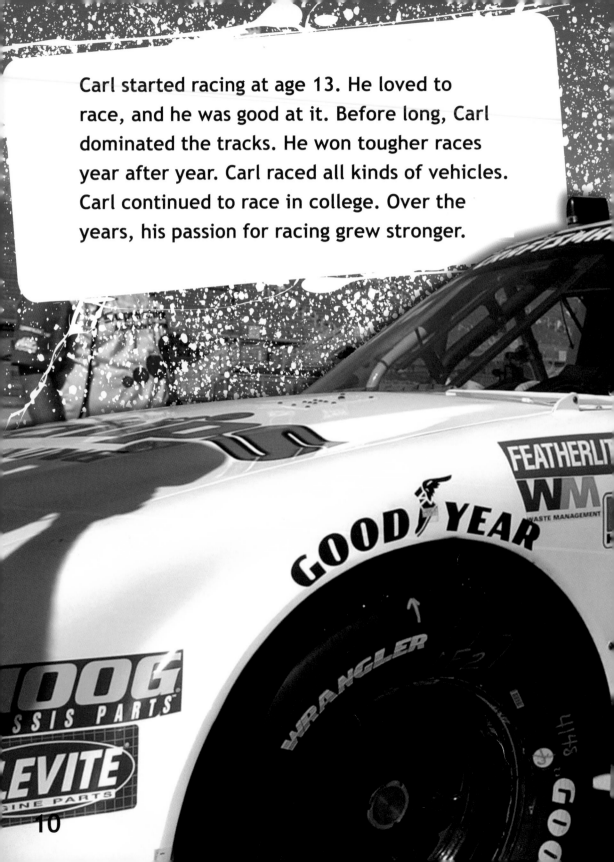

Carl started racing at age 13. He loved to race, and he was good at it. Before long, Carl dominated the tracks. He won tougher races year after year. Carl raced all kinds of vehicles. Carl continued to race in college. Over the years, his passion for racing grew stronger.

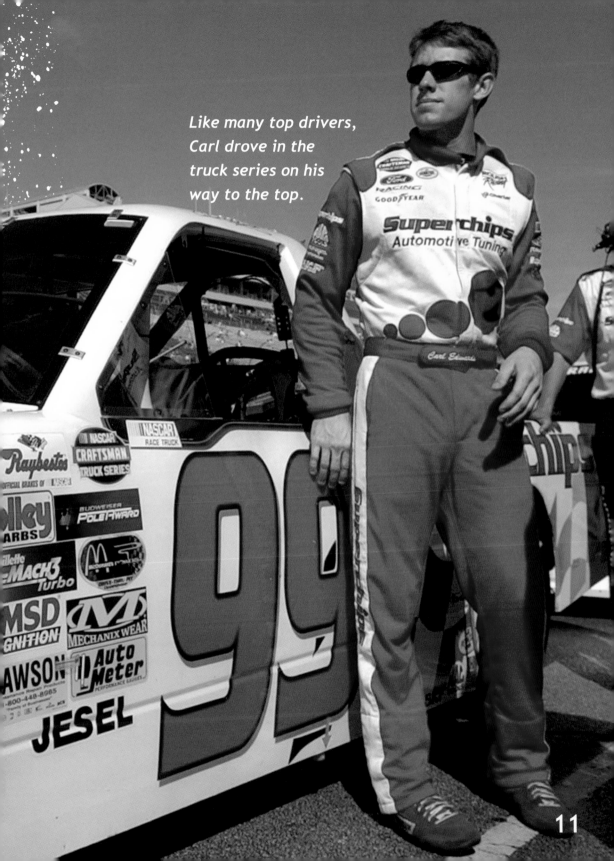

Like many top drivers, Carl drove in the truck series on his way to the top.

DISCOVERED!

Edwards was determined to become a NASCAR driver. He printed business cards with the title "Race Car Driver." He gave them to NASCAR team owners. He called owners on the phone. He did everything he could to get noticed.

Finally, in 2003, someone noticed. NASCAR owner Jack Roush liked Edwards's passion and skill on the track. Roush invited Edwards to join his Roush Fenway Racing Team.

Edwards flips out after winning a truck race in 2004.

13

In August 2004, Edwards was slotted to race in NASCAR's Cup Series. He was nervous, but he proved ready for the challenge. In his first race, he finished in tenth place out of 43 racers. He finished in the top 10 four more times that year.

FAST FACT

Carl Edwards is one of only five racers to finish in the top 10 in his first NASCAR Cup Series start.

Edwards leads a line of cars during a 2004 race in Bristol, Tennessee.

Edwards celebrates a win in 2005 at Texas Motor Speedway.

A BIG FIRST YEAR

Edwards's first full year as a NASCAR driver was in 2005. He raced in both the Cup and second-level series. In the Cup Series, Edwards finished third. He had four wins and 13 top-five finishes. On the second level, he had five wins, four poles, and 15 top-five finishes. He was named the second level's Rookie of the Year.

18

THE RACE GOES ON

Fans at Atlanta Motor Speedway saw something amazing in 2005. In the same weekend, Edwards won both his first Cup Series and second-level races. No NASCAR driver in history had ever done that.

Edwards celebrates with owner Jack Roush after winning two races in one weekend in 2005.

Edwards and his crew had a lot to celebrate during his rookie Cup Series season in 2005.

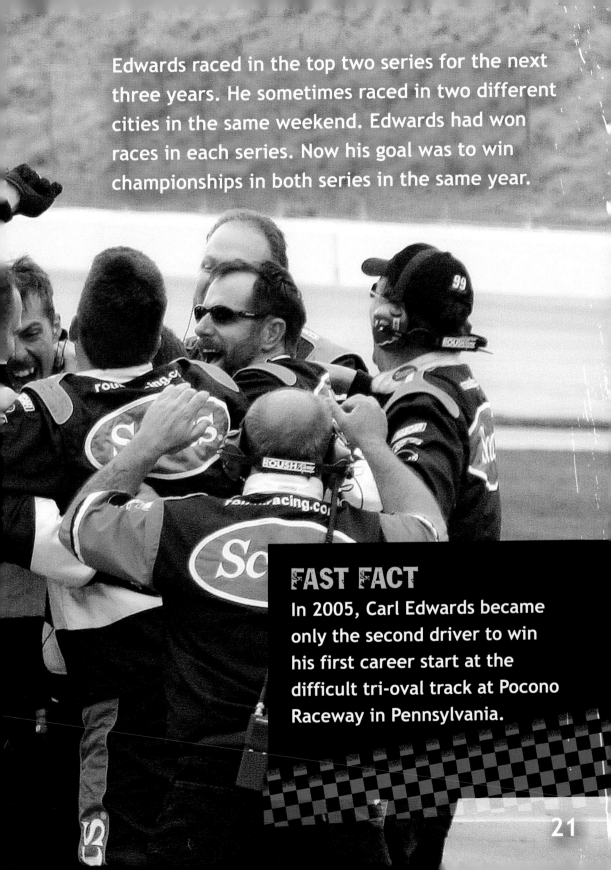

Edwards raced in the top two series for the next three years. He sometimes raced in two different cities in the same weekend. Edwards had won races in each series. Now his goal was to win championships in both series in the same year.

FAST FACT

In 2005, Carl Edwards became only the second driver to win his first career start at the difficult tri-oval track at Pocono Raceway in Pennsylvania.

Edwards celebrates after winning a race in 2010 in Homestead, Florida.

In 2007, Edwards met part of this goal. He won the second-level championship. Edwards also had strong years in 2008, 2009, and 2010. In 2008, he moved even closer to his goal. He came in second place in both series.

FAST FACT

Carl Edwards married Katherine Downey on January 3, 2009. They have a daughter named Anne and a son named Michael.

A TRUE SUPERSTAR

Edwards is one of the most competitive racers in NASCAR. He continues to edge closer to championship wins every year. In 2011, Edwards again almost won the top-level Sprint Cup Series championship. He lost in a tiebreaker. Still, Edwards led the series in top-five and top-10 finishes.

Edwards (99) cruises during a 2011 race in Sparta, Kentucky.

FAST FACT

As of 2011, Carl Edwards had finished in the top 10 in the Sprint Cup Series five times.

The pit crew works on
Edwards's car during a 2012
race in North Carolina.

MORE TO COME

In 2011, Edwards had to rethink his racing goal. New rules stated that no driver could win championships in both series in the same year. So in 2012, Edwards decided not to race in the second-level Nationwide Series. He focused on the Sprint Cup Series instead.

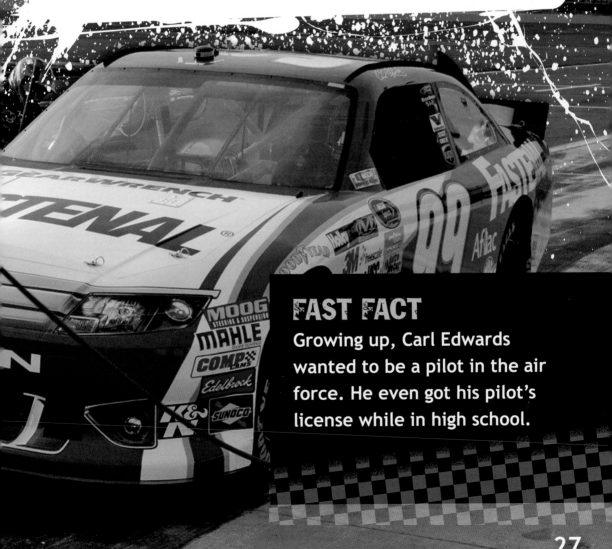

FAST FACT
Growing up, Carl Edwards wanted to be a pilot in the air force. He even got his pilot's license while in high school.

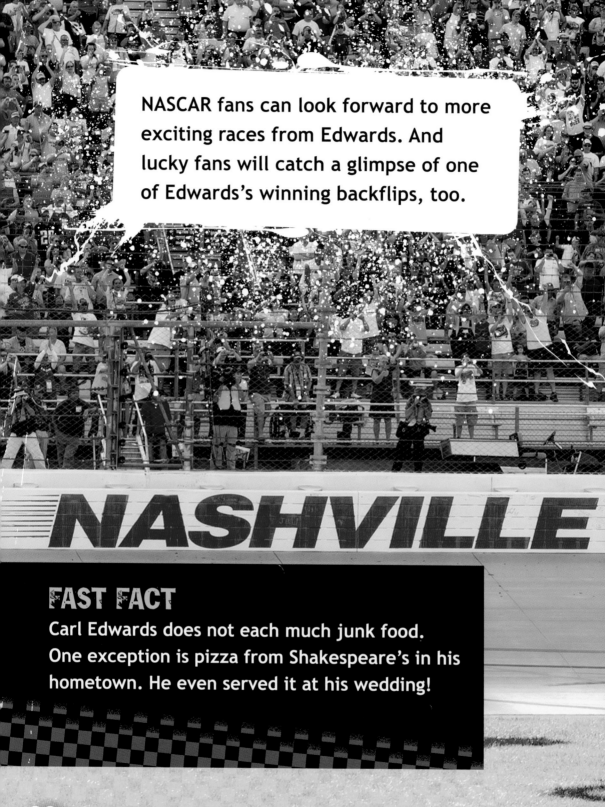

NASCAR fans can look forward to more exciting races from Edwards. And lucky fans will catch a glimpse of one of Edwards's winning backflips, too.

FAST FACT

Carl Edwards does not each much junk food. One exception is pizza from Shakespeare's in his hometown. He even served it at his wedding!

SUPERSPEEDV

With some good driving, more celebratory backflips could be in store for Edwards.

TIMELINE

1979

Carl Edwards is born on August 15 in Columbia, Missouri.

2003

Edwards joins Roush Fenway Racing Team.

2005

Edwards gets his first big win in NASCAR on March 20.

2007

Edwards wins NASCAR's second-level series title.

2008

Edwards comes in second place in both of NASCAR's top series.

2009

Edwards marries Katherine Downey.

2011

Edwards almost wins the NASCAR Sprint Cup Series. He finishes second in a tiebreaker.

2012

Edwards opts out of the NASCAR Nationwide Series to focus on the Sprint Cup Series.

GLOSSARY

Cup Series
NASCAR's top series for professional stock car drivers. It has been called the Sprint Cup Series since 2008.

midgets
Small race cars designed for short races.

owner
The person who owns an entire racing team. This person hires everyone on the team, including the driver and the pit crew.

pole
The car with the fastest time in qualifying; this car starts first in a race.

rookie
A driver in his or her first full-time season in a new series.

second-level series
NASCAR's second-level series for professional stock car drivers. It has been called the Nationwide Series since 2008.

series
A racing season that consists of several races.

start
Races in which the driver participates from the beginning.

stock car
Race cars that resemble models of cars that people drive every day.

INDEX

24, 16

Atlanta Motor
   Speedway, 4, 19

Backflips, 6, 7, 13,
   28, 29

College, 9, 10
Columbia, Missouri,
   8-9
Cup Series, 5, 6, 7,
   14, 15, 17, 19, 20,
   21, 23, 24, 25, 27

Downey, Katherine,
   23

Early career, 10, 12
Edheads, 5

Family, 8, 23
favorite food, 28
first win, 4-7

Growing up, 8, 27

Johnson, Jimmie, 5

Kids, 23

National Association
for Stock Car Auto
Racing (NASCAR),
6, 7, 12, 14, 15, 17,
19, 24, 28

Pilot, 27
pit crew, 20, 26
Pocono Raceway, 21

Rookie of the Year,
   17
Roush Fenway
   Racing, 12
Roush, Jack, 12, 19

Second-level
   championship, 23
second-level series,
   17, 19, 21, 23, 27

Texas Motor
   Speedway, 16
trucks series, 11, 13

University of
   Missouri, 9

J B Edwards, Carl

Carl Edwards   AUGu1 ъъ X

Miller, Connie Colwell.
$27.07   3201200050665